AED

INSPECTION LOGBOOK

MONTHLY AED MAINTENANCE AND INSPECTION RECORD
FOR WORKPLACES, SCHOOLS, GYMS, AND PUBLIC FACILITIES

Ebony Godwin, RN, BSN, M.S.

This publication is intended for personal use and general information purposes only. It does not constitute medical advice, diagnosis, or treatment. Always consult a licensed healthcare provider for medical concerns. The publisher and author disclaim any liability for actions taken based on the contents of this book.

PUBLISHED BY ADALYNN JAMES
Cincinnati, OH 45242, USA
www.adalynnjames.com
connect@adalynnjames.com

ADALYNN JAMES

Ordering Information
Quantity purchase options are available for schools, businesses, conferences, and organizations interested in group copies. For details, please get in touch with the publisher at the email address above.

ISBN: 978-1-968371-07-4

Table of Contents

Welcome	5
Emergency Contact	11
AED Device Inventory	12
Authorized Inspectors	13
CPR/AED Certification Tracker	15
Incident Occurrence Record	21
AED Monthly Inspection Checklist	27
Replacement Log	41
Troubleshooting Notes	53
Annual AED Inspection Summary	63
Closing Message	77
About the Author	78
Share Your Experience	79

Welcome

Sudden cardiac arrest can occur anywhere, including offices, schools, gyms, warehouses, retail spaces, and community facilities. An Automated External Defibrillator (AED) can save a life, but only if the device is ready when it is needed.

This AED Maintenance Tracker Logbook was created to help organizations maintain their AEDs with consistency, accountability, and clear documentation.

This logbook provides a centralized system to:

- Document AED inspections
- Track equipment readiness
- Record maintenance and component replacements
- Maintain organized records for compliance and accountability

Consistent documentation supports workplace safety programs and helps organizations demonstrate due diligence while maintaining a reliable emergency response environment.

Why AED Readiness Matters

When a cardiac emergency occurs, there is no time to troubleshoot equipment, search for supplies, or determine who is responsible to respond.

Delays in accessing a working AED can significantly reduce the chance of survival. Even a short delay caused by missing equipment, expired pads, or an unrecognized device issue can impact the outcome.

Many organizations install AEDs with good intentions but lack a consistent system to ensure the device remains ready for use. Over time, this can lead to:

- Expired pads or batteries going unnoticed
- Missing or incomplete rescue kits
- Equipment stored in inaccessible locations
- Uncertainty about who is responsible for inspections

AED readiness is not just about having the device. It is about maintaining a system that ensures the device is functional, accessible, and ready to be used without hesitation. A structured readiness program helps reduce confusion, supports faster response, and ensures the equipment performs as expected during an emergency.

AED Inspection Frequency Guidelines

Routine inspections are a critical part of maintaining AED readiness.

Most organizations perform monthly visual inspections to confirm that the device is functional, accessible, and properly maintained.

Assigning clear responsibility for inspections helps ensure consistency and accountability within your safety program

.

During each inspection, designated staff should verify:

- The AED status indicator shows "ready"
- Electrode pads are sealed and within expiration date
- Battery is installed and within expiration date
- Rescue kit is complete and stocked
- AED location is clearly visible and accessible
- Cabinet alarm and signage are functioning (if applicable)

Any issues identified during inspection should be addressed promptly and documented within this logbook.

Consistent inspections and accurate recordkeeping help organizations maintain readiness, support compliance efforts, and ensure the AED is prepared for use when needed.

How to Use This Logbook

1. Assign Responsible Inspectors

Designate staff members responsible for performing routine AED inspections.

2. Record Device Information

Use the AED Inventory page to document each device within your facility.

3. Complete Monthly Inspections

Perform a visual inspection each month and record results in the inspection tracker.

4. Document Equipment Changes

Record pad replacements, battery replacements, and any maintenance or service events.

5. Record Incident Occurrences

If the AED is used during an emergency, document the event for follow-up and readiness review.

AED Program Essentials

AED programs should include:

- Clearly visible and accessible AED placement
- Routine equipment inspections
- Fully stocked rescue kits
- Documented maintenance records
- Staff awareness or trained responders

Maintaining these elements helps ensure the device is ready if an emergency occurs.

Typical AED Inspection Checklist

Inspectors should confirm:

- AED location signage is visible
- Cabinet alarm is functioning (if applicable)
- Rescue kit is stocked and complete
- Battery is installed and within expiration date
- Electrode pads are sealed and not expired
- Status indicator shows the device is ready

Notes

EMERGENCY CONTACT & RESPONSE INFORMATION

SECTION 1 — FACILITY INFORMATION

Facility / Organization Name: ______________________________

Facility Address: ______________________________
(for 911 Dispatch)

City / State / ZIP: ______________________________

SECTION 2 — AED INFORMATION

AED Location (Primary): ______________________________

(Secondary) AED Location: ______________________________

SECTION 3 — EMERGENCY CONTACTS

Primary Contact
Name: ______________
Title: ______________
Phone: ______________

Secondary Contact
Name: ______________
Title: ______________
Phone: ______________

SECTION 4 — EMERGENCY SERVICES

Emergency Number (911): ______________
Nearest Hospital Name: ______________
Estimated Drive Time: ______________

Non-Emergency Number: ______________
Hospital Phone: ______________

SECTION 5 — EMERGENCY EQUIPMENT LOCATIONS

First Aid Kit Location: ______________
Bleeding Control Kit Location: ______________

SECTION 6 — EMS ACCESS INSTRUCTIONS

Best Entrance for EMS: ______________
Special Instructions / Access Codes: ______________

IN CASE OF CARDIAC EMERGENCY — ACT IMMEDIATELY

1. Call 911 immediately.
2. Begin CPR if the person is unresponsive and not breathing normally.
3. Retrieve the nearest AED and power it on.
4. Follow all AED audio and visual prompts.
5. Direct EMS to the exact location upon arrival.

SECTION 8 — REVIEW & APPROVAL

Last Updated: ______________ Reviewed By: ______________

Last Updated: ______________ Reviewed By: ______________

BE PREPARED. STAY READY. SAVE LIVES.

AED Device Inventory

Use this page to record the location and basic details of every AED within your facility. This helps your safety team assign inspections, track equipment readiness, and ensure each device is easy to locate during an emergency.

AED Location	Device ID/Serial No.	Expiration Dates (Pads/Battery)	Notes

Authorized Inspectors

This page records the names and contact information of the individuals authorized to inspect and maintain the Automated External Defibrillator (AED) unit. Each person listed here should be trained in AED operation and understand the monthly inspection process.

Name	Title/Role	Phone/Email	Initials

(Add or update names as your team changes. All inspectors should review the AED checklist before completing their first inspection.)

Authorized Inspectors

This page records the names and contact information of the individuals authorized to inspect and maintain the Automated External Defibrillator (AED) unit. Each person listed here should be trained in AED operation and understand the monthly inspection process.

Name	Title/Role	Phone/Email	Initials

(Add or update names as your team changes. All inspectors should review the AED checklist before completing their first inspection.)

CPR/AED Certification Tracker

Use this page to track CPR and AED certifications for members of your facility's emergency response or safety team. This helps ensure ongoing readiness and allows for proactive renewal planning.

Most CPR and AED certifications expire every 2 years. Check with your certification provider for renewal requirements and timelines.

Team Member Name	Role	Certification Type	Provider	Certification Date	Expiration Date	Notes/Renewal Plan

CPR/AED Certification Tracker

Use this page to track CPR and AED certifications for members of your facility's emergency response or safety team. This helps ensure ongoing readiness and allows for proactive renewal planning.

Most CPR and AED certifications expire every 2 years. Check with your certification provider for renewal requirements and timelines.

Team Member Name	Role	Certification Type	Provider	Certification Date	Expiration Date	Notes/Renewal Plan

CPR/AED Certification Tracker

Use this page to track CPR and AED certifications for members of your facility's emergency response or safety team. This helps ensure ongoing readiness and allows for proactive renewal planning.

Most CPR and AED certifications expire every 2 years. Check with your certification provider for renewal requirements and timelines.

Team Member Name	Role	Certification Type	Provider	Certification Date	Expiration Date	Notes/Renewal Plan

CPR/AED Certification Tracker

Use this page to track CPR and AED certifications for members of your facility's emergency response or safety team. This helps ensure ongoing readiness and allows for proactive renewal planning.

Most CPR and AED certifications expire every 2 years. Check with your certification provider for renewal requirements and timelines.

Team Member Name	Role	Certification Type	Provider	Certification Date	Expiration Date	Notes/Renewal Plan

CPR/AED Certification Tracker

Use this page to track CPR and AED certifications for members of your facility's emergency response or safety team. This helps ensure ongoing readiness and allows for proactive renewal planning.

Most CPR and AED certifications expire every 2 years. Check with your certification provider for renewal requirements and timelines.

Team Member Name	Role	Certification Type	Provider	Certification Date	Expiration Date	Notes/Renewal Plan

Notes

Incident Occurrence Record (Reference Only)

Instructions:

Use this page to record when a medical incident involving the AED occurs. This record is for reference and accountability only.

Do not include personal medical details, names, or outcomes on this page. Complete any detailed incident documentation using your organization's secure reporting process.

This page helps ensure follow-up actions, equipment checks, and leadership awareness.

Date	AED Unit (Location or ID)	Incident Location	AED Deployed (Yes/No)	Emergency Services Contacted? (Yes/No)	Incident Report Completed? (Yes/No)	Location of Incident Report (online system)

Incident Occurrence Record (Reference Only)

Instructions:

Use this page to record when a medical incident involving the AED occurs. This record is for reference and accountability only.

Do not include personal medical details, names, or outcomes on this page. Complete any detailed incident documentation using your organization's secure reporting process.

This page helps ensure follow-up actions, equipment checks, and leadership awareness.

Date	AED Unit (Location or ID)	Incident Location	AED Deployed (Yes/No)	Emergency Services Contacted? (Yes/No)	Incident Report Completed? (Yes/No)	Location of Incident Report (online system)

Incident Occurrence Record (Reference Only)

Instructions:

Use this page to record when a medical incident involving the AED occurs. This record is for reference and accountability only.

Do not include personal medical details, names, or outcomes on this page. Complete any detailed incident documentation using your organization's secure reporting process.

This page helps ensure follow-up actions, equipment checks, and leadership awareness.

Date	AED Unit (Location or ID)	Incident Location	AED Deployed (Yes/No)	Emergency Services Contacted? (Yes/No)	Incident Report Completed? (Yes/No)	Location of Incident Report (online system)

Incident Occurrence Record (Reference Only)

Instructions:

Use this page to record when a medical incident involving the AED occurs. This record is for reference and accountability only.

Do not include personal medical details, names, or outcomes on this page. Complete any detailed incident documentation using your organization's secure reporting process.

This page helps ensure follow-up actions, equipment checks, and leadership awareness.

Date	AED Unit (Location or ID)	Incident Location	AED Deployed (Yes/No)	Emergency Services Contacted? (Yes/No)	Incident Report Completed? (Yes/No)	Location of Incident Report (online system)

Incident Occurrence Record (Reference Only)

Instructions:

Use this page to record when a medical incident involving the AED occurs. This record is for reference and accountability only.

Do not include personal medical details, names, or outcomes on this page. Complete any detailed incident documentation using your organization's secure reporting process.

This page helps ensure follow-up actions, equipment checks, and leadership awareness.

Date	AED Unit (Location or ID)	Incident Location	AED Deployed (Yes/No)	Emergency Services Contacted? (Yes/No)	Incident Report Completed? (Yes/No)	Location of Incident Report (online system)

Notes

Year: ____________

AED (Automated External Defibrillator) Monthly Inspection Checklist

- To be completed by the CPR attendant and posted near the AED unit
- To be completed every month and when taken out for any emergency event
- Checkmark blank box only if the item passes; if it fails, do not initial until the problem is fixed
- When the key is in the off position, the cabinet should open with no alarm

AED Location/
Device ID: ____________

	Month (Initial in each box upon inspection)											
	January	February	March	April	May	June	July	August	September	October	November	December
AED condition: No dirt, damage or contamination												
Ensure that the device ready status indicator is displayed (Green Checkmark)												
Ensure that pads are still good (Check expiration date, Pad packaging is sealed)												
Ensure that the batteries are still operational on AED (Remove to check once a year)												
Ensure the wall cabinet alarm is sounding and the red light is flashing (Check alarm battery)												
Ensure you have a rescue kit ready (Scissors, Face Mask, Razor, Disposable Gloves etc.)												
Alarm key present and functioning												
Cabinet is secure to the wall												
Ensure: Fire Extinguisher Location & Accessibility, Labels, Pressure Gauge, Not expired, Hose intact, Pin in place, Inspection Tag, Secure to the wall												
Remarks/Problems/Corrective Actions												
Initial of person who completed inspection												

If the AED does not pass inspection, follow the troubleshooting instructions in the manual provided. If the issue can't be resolved, please contact ____________ at ____________.

Year: ______________

AED (Automated External Defibrillator) Monthly Inspection Checklist

- To be completed by the CPR attendant and posted near the AED unit
- To be completed every month and when taken out for any emergency event
- Checkmark blank box only if the item passes; if it fails, do not initial until the problem is fixed
- When the key is in the off position, the cabinet should open with no alarm

AED Location/
Device ID: ______________________

	Month (Initial in each box upon inspection)											
	January	February	March	April	May	June	July	August	September	October	November	December
AED condition: No dirt, damage or contamination												
Ensure that the device ready status indicator is displayed (Green Checkmark)												
Ensure that pads are still good (Check expiration date, Pad packaging is sealed)												
Ensure that the batteries are still operational on AED (Remove to check once a year)												
Ensure the wall cabinet alarm is sounding and the red light is flashing (Check alarm battery)												
Ensure you have a rescue kit ready (Scissors, Face Mask, Razor, Disposable Gloves etc.)												
Alarm key present and functioning												
Cabinet is secure to the wall												
Ensure: Fire Extinguisher Location & Accessibility, Labels, Pressure Gauge, Not expired, Hose intact, Pin in place, Inspection Tag, Secure to the wall												
Remarks/Problems/Corrective Actions												
Initial of person who completed inspection												

If the AED does not pass inspection, follow the troubleshooting instructions in the manual provided. If the issue can't be resolved, please contact ______________ at ______________.

Year: ______________

AED (Automated External Defibrillator) Monthly Inspection Checklist

- To be completed by the CPR attendant and posted near the AED unit
- To be completed every month and when taken out for any emergency event
- Checkmark blank box only if the item passes; if it fails, do not initial until the problem is fixed
- When the key is in the off position, the cabinet should open with no alarm

AED Location/
Device ID: ____________________

	Month (Initial in each box upon inspection)											
	January	February	March	April	May	June	July	August	September	October	November	December
AED condition: No dirt, damage or contamination												
Ensure that the device ready status indicator is displayed (Green Checkmark)												
Ensure that pads are still good (Check expiration date, Pad packaging is sealed)												
Ensure that the batteries are still operational on AED (Remove to check once a year)												
Ensure the wall cabinet alarm is sounding and the red light is flashing (Check alarm battery)												
Ensure you have a rescue kit ready (Scissors, Face Mask, Razor, Disposable Gloves etc.)												
Alarm key present and functioning												
Cabinet is secure to the wall												
Ensure: Fire Extinguisher Location & Accessibility, Labels, Pressure Gauge, Not expired, Hose intact, Pin in place, Inspection Tag, Secure to the wall												
Remarks/Problems/Corrective Actions												
Initial of person who completed inspection												

If the AED does not pass inspection, follow the troubleshooting instructions in the manual provided. If the issue can't be resolved, please contact ______________________ at ______________________.

Year: ______________

AED (Automated External Defibrillator) Monthly Inspection Checklist

- To be completed by the CPR attendant and posted near the AED unit
- To be completed every month and when taken out for any emergency event
- Checkmark blank box only if the item passes; if it fails, do not initial until the problem is fixed
- When the key is in the off position, the cabinet should open with no alarm

AED Location/
Device ID: ____________________________

	Month (Initial in each box upon inspection)											
	January	February	March	April	May	June	July	August	September	October	November	December
AED condition: No dirt, damage or contamination												
Ensure that the device ready status indicator is displayed (Green Checkmark)												
Ensure that pads are still good (Check expiration date, Pad packaging is sealed)												
Ensure that the batteries are still operational on AED (Remove to check once a year)												
Ensure the wall cabinet alarm is sounding and the red light is flashing (Check alarm battery)												
Ensure you have a rescue kit ready (Scissors, Face Mask, Razor, Disposable Gloves etc.)												
Alarm key present and functioning												
Cabinet is secure to the wall												
Ensure: Fire Extinguisher Location & Accessibility, Labels, Pressure Gauge, Not expired, Hose intact, Pin in place, Inspection Tag, Secure to the wall												
Remarks/Problems/Corrective Actions												
Initial of person who completed inspection												

If the AED does not pass inspection, follow the troubleshooting instructions in the manual provided. If the issue can't be resolved, please contact
at .

Year: ______________ **AED (Automated External Defibrillator) Monthly Inspection Checklist**

- To be completed by the CPR attendant and posted near the AED unit
- To be completed every month and when taken out for any emergency event
- Checkmark blank box only if the item passes; if it fails, do not initial until the problem is fixed
- When the key is in the off position, the cabinet should open with no alarm

AED Location/
Device ID: ______________________________

	Month (Initial in each box upon inspection)											
	January	February	March	April	May	June	July	August	September	October	November	December
AED condition: No dirt, damage or contamination												
Ensure that the device ready status indicator is displayed (Green Checkmark)												
Ensure that pads are still good (Check expiration date, Pad packaging is sealed)												
Ensure that the batteries are still operational on AED (Remove to check once a year)												
Ensure the wall cabinet alarm is sounding and the red light is flashing (Check alarm battery)												
Ensure you have a rescue kit ready (Scissors, Face Mask, Razor, Disposable Gloves etc.)												
Alarm key present and functioning												
Cabinet is secure to the wall												
Ensure: Fire Extinguisher Location & Accessibility, Labels, Pressure Gauge, Not expired, Hose intact, Pin in place, Inspection Tag, Secure to the wall												
Remarks/Problems/Corrective Actions												
Initial of person who completed inspection												

If the AED does not pass inspection, follow the troubleshooting instructions in the manual provided. If the issue can't be resolved, please contact ______________________________ at ______________________________.

Year: ______________

AED (Automated External Defibrillator) Monthly Inspection Checklist

- To be completed by the CPR attendant and posted near the AED unit
- To be completed every month and when taken out for any emergency event
- Checkmark blank box only if the item passes; if it fails, do not initial until the problem is fixed
- When the key is in the off position, the cabinet should open with no alarm

AED Location/
Device ID: ______________________________

	Month (Initial in each box upon inspection)											
	January	February	March	April	May	June	July	August	September	October	November	December
AED condition: No dirt, damage or contamination												
Ensure that the device ready status indicator is displayed (Green Checkmark)												
Ensure that pads are still good (Check expiration date, Pad packaging is sealed)												
Ensure that the batteries are still operational on AED (Remove to check once a year)												
Ensure the wall cabinet alarm is sounding and the red light is flashing (Check alarm battery)												
Ensure you have a rescue kit ready (Scissors, Face Mask, Razor, Disposable Gloves etc.)												
Alarm key present and functioning												
Cabinet is secure to the wall												
Ensure: Fire Extinguisher Location & Accessibility, Labels, Pressure Gauge, Not expired, Hose intact, Pin in place, Inspection Tag, Secure to the wall												
Remarks/Problems/Corrective Actions												
Initial of person who completed inspection												

If the AED does not pass inspection, follow the troubleshooting instructions in the manual provided. If the issue can't be resolved, please contact ____________________ at ____________________.

Year: ______________

AED (Automated External Defibrillator) Monthly Inspection Checklist

AED Location/
Device ID: ____________________________

- To be completed by the CPR attendant and posted near the AED unit
- To be completed every month and when taken out for any emergency event
- Checkmark blank box only if the item passes; if it fails, do not initial until the problem is fixed
- When the key is in the off position, the cabinet should open with no alarm

	Month (Initial in each box upon inspection)											
	January	February	March	April	May	June	July	August	September	October	November	December
AED condition: No dirt, damage or contamination												
Ensure that the device ready status indicator is displayed (Green Checkmark)												
Ensure that pads are still good (Check expiration date, Pad packaging is sealed)												
Ensure that the batteries are still operational on AED (Remove to check once a year)												
Ensure the wall cabinet alarm is sounding and the red light is flashing (Check alarm battery)												
Ensure you have a rescue kit ready (Scissors, Face Mask, Razor, Disposable Gloves etc.)												
Alarm key present and functioning												
Cabinet is secure to the wall												
Ensure: Fire Extinguisher Location & Accessibility, Labels, Pressure Gauge, Not expired, Hose intact, Pin in place, Inspection Tag, Secure to the wall												
Remarks/Problems/Corrective Actions												
Initial of person who completed inspection												

If the AED does not pass inspection, follow the troubleshooting instructions in the manual provided. If the issue can't be resolved, please contact ______________________________ at ______________________________.

Year: ______________

AED (Automated External Defibrillator) Monthly Inspection Checklist

- To be completed by the CPR attendant and posted near the AED unit
- To be completed every month and when taken out for any emergency event
- Checkmark blank box only if the item passes; if it fails, do not initial until the problem is fixed
- When the key is in the off position, the cabinet should open with no alarm

AED Location/
Device ID: ______________________________

	Month (Initial in each box upon inspection)											
	January	February	March	April	May	June	July	August	September	October	November	December
AED condition: No dirt, damage or contamination												
Ensure that the device ready status indicator is displayed (Green Checkmark)												
Ensure that pads are still good (Check expiration date, Pad packaging is sealed)												
Ensure that the batteries are still operational on AED (Remove to check once a year)												
Ensure the wall cabinet alarm is sounding and the red light is flashing (Check alarm battery)												
Ensure you have a rescue kit ready (Scissors, Face Mask, Razor, Disposable Gloves etc.)												
Alarm key present and functioning												
Cabinet is secure to the wall												
Ensure: Fire Extinguisher Location & Accessibility, Labels, Pressure Gauge, Not expired, Hose intact, Pin in place, Inspection Tag, Secure to the wall												
Remarks/Problems/Corrective Actions												
Initial of person who completed inspection												

If the AED does not pass inspection, follow the troubleshooting instructions in the manual provided. If the issue can't be resolved, please contact
at

Year: ______________

AED (Automated External Defibrillator) Monthly Inspection Checklist

- To be completed by the CPR attendant and posted near the AED unit
- To be completed every month and when taken out for any emergency event
- Checkmark blank box only if the item passes; if it fails, do not initial until the problem is fixed
- When the key is in the off position, the cabinet should open with no alarm

AED Location/
Device ID: ______________________________

	Month (Initial in each box upon inspection)											
	January	February	March	April	May	June	July	August	September	October	November	December
AED condition: No dirt, damage or contamination												
Ensure that the device ready status indicator is displayed (Green Checkmark)												
Ensure that pads are still good (Check expiration date, Pad packaging is sealed)												
Ensure that the batteries are still operational on AED (Remove to check once a year)												
Ensure the wall cabinet alarm is sounding and the red light is flashing (Check alarm battery)												
Ensure you have a rescue kit ready (Scissors, Face Mask, Razor, Disposable Gloves etc.)												
Alarm key present and functioning												
Cabinet is secure to the wall												
Ensure: Fire Extinguisher Location & Accessibility, Labels, Pressure Gauge, Not expired, Hose intact, Pin in place, Inspection Tag, Secure to the wall												
Remarks/Problems/Corrective Actions												
Initial of person who completed inspection												

If the AED does not pass inspection, follow the troubleshooting instructions in the manual provided. If the issue can't be resolved, please contact ______________________________ at ______________________________.

Year: ______________

AED (Automated External Defibrillator) Monthly Inspection Checklist

AED Location/
Device ID: ______________________

- To be completed by the CPR attendant and posted near the AED unit
- To be completed every month and when taken out for any emergency event
- Checkmark blank box only if the item passes; if it fails, do not initial until the problem is fixed
- When the key is in the off position, the cabinet should open with no alarm

	Month (Initial in each box upon inspection)											
	January	February	March	April	May	June	July	August	September	October	November	December
AED condition: No dirt, damage or contamination												
Ensure that the device ready status indicator is displayed (Green Checkmark)												
Ensure that pads are still good (Check expiration date, Pad packaging is sealed)												
Ensure that the batteries are still operational on AED (Remove to check once a year)												
Ensure the wall cabinet alarm is sounding and the red light is flashing (Check alarm battery)												
Ensure you have a rescue kit ready (Scissors, Face Mask, Razor, Disposable Gloves etc.)												
Alarm key present and functioning												
Cabinet is secure to the wall												
Ensure: Fire Extinguisher Location & Accessibility, Labels, Pressure Gauge, Not expired, Hose intact, Pin in place, Inspection Tag, Secure to the wall												
Remarks/Problems/Corrective Actions												
Initial of person who completed inspection												

If the AED does not pass inspection, follow the troubleshooting instructions in the manual provided. If the issue can't be resolved, please contact ______________________ at ______________________.

Year: ______________

AED (Automated External Defibrillator) Monthly Inspection Checklist

AED Location/
Device ID: ______________________________

- To be completed by the CPR attendant and posted near the AED unit
- To be completed every month and when taken out for any emergency event
- Checkmark blank box only if the item passes; if it fails, do not initial until the problem is fixed
- When the key is in the off position, the cabinet should open with no alarm

	Month (Initial in each box upon inspection)											
	January	February	March	April	May	June	July	August	September	October	November	December
AED condition: No dirt, damage or contamination												
Ensure that the device ready status indicator is displayed (Green Checkmark)												
Ensure that pads are still good (Check expiration date, Pad packaging is sealed)												
Ensure that the batteries are still operational on AED (Remove to check once a year)												
Ensure the wall cabinet alarm is sounding and the red light is flashing (Check alarm battery)												
Ensure you have a rescue kit ready (Scissors, Face Mask, Razor, Disposable Gloves etc.)												
Alarm key present and functioning												
Cabinet is secure to the wall												
Ensure: Fire Extinguisher Location & Accessibility, Labels, Pressure Gauge, Not expired, Hose intact, Pin in place, Inspection Tag, Secure to the wall												
Remarks/Problems/Corrective Actions												
Initial of person who completed inspection												

If the AED does not pass inspection, follow the troubleshooting instructions in the manual provided. If the issue can't be resolved, please contact ______________________________ at ______________________________.

Year: ______________ **AED (Automated External Defibrillator) Monthly Inspection Checklist**

- To be completed by the CPR attendant and posted near the AED unit
- To be completed every month and when taken out for any emergency event
- Checkmark blank box only if the item passes; if it fails, do not initial until the problem is fixed
- When the key is in the off position, the cabinet should open with no alarm

AED Location/
Device ID: ______________________

	Month (Initial in each box upon inspection)											
	January	February	March	April	May	June	July	August	September	October	November	December
AED condition: No dirt, damage or contamination												
Ensure that the device ready status indicator is displayed (Green Checkmark)												
Ensure that pads are still good (Check expiration date, Pad packaging is sealed)												
Ensure that the batteries are still operational on AED (Remove to check once a year)												
Ensure the wall cabinet alarm is sounding and the red light is flashing (Check alarm battery)												
Ensure you have a rescue kit ready (Scissors, Face Mask, Razor, Disposable Gloves etc.)												
Alarm key present and functioning												
Cabinet is secure to the wall												
Ensure: Fire Extinguisher Location & Accessibility, Labels, Pressure Gauge, Not expired, Hose intact, Pin in place, Inspection Tag, Secure to the wall												
Remarks/Problems/Corrective Actions												
Initial of person who completed inspection												

If the AED does not pass inspection, follow the troubleshooting instructions in the manual provided. If the issue can't be resolved, please contact
at

Notes

Notes

Replacement Log

Use this page to record every replacement or update of AED components, including pads, batteries, rescue kit items, or accessories for each device.

If your organization maintains more than one AED, record the AED location or device number in the second column to ensure clear tracking.

Date	AED Location / Device ID	Item Replaced	Reason for Replacement	Replaced By (Name / Initials)	Next Replacement Due	Remarks

(Tip: Record pad expirations, battery replacements, alarm battery changes, and rescue kit restocks here. For multi-AED campuses, assign a simple device label such as "AED #1—Front Lobby," "AED #2—2nd Floor Hallway," etc.)

Replacement Log

Use this page to record every replacement or update of AED components, including pads, batteries, rescue kit items, or accessories for each device.

If your organization maintains more than one AED, record the AED location or device number in the second column to ensure clear tracking.

Date	AED Location / Device ID	Item Replaced	Reason for Replacement	Replaced By (Name / Initials)	Next Replacement Due	Remarks

(Tip: Record pad expirations, battery replacements, alarm battery changes, and rescue kit restocks here. For multi-AED campuses, assign a simple device label such as "AED #1—Front Lobby," "AED #2—2nd Floor Hallway," etc.)

Replacement Log

Use this page to record every replacement or update of AED components, including pads, batteries, rescue kit items, or accessories for each device.

If your organization maintains more than one AED, record the AED location or device number in the second column to ensure clear tracking.

Date	AED Location / Device ID	Item Replaced	Reason for Replacement	Replaced By (Name / Initials)	Next Replacement Due	Remarks

(Tip: Record pad expirations, battery replacements, alarm battery changes, and rescue kit restocks here. For multi-AED campuses, assign a simple device label such as "AED #1—Front Lobby," "AED #2—2nd Floor Hallway," etc.)

Replacement Log

Use this page to record every replacement or update of AED components, including pads, batteries, rescue kit items, or accessories for each device.

If your organization maintains more than one AED, record the AED location or device number in the second column to ensure clear tracking.

Date	AED Location / Device ID	Item Replaced	Reason for Replacement	Replaced By (Name / Initials)	Next Replacement Due	Remarks

(Tip: Record pad expirations, battery replacements, alarm battery changes, and rescue kit restocks here. For multi-AED campuses, assign a simple device label such as "AED #1—Front Lobby," "AED #2—2nd Floor Hallway," etc.)

Replacement Log

Use this page to record every replacement or update of AED components, including pads, batteries, rescue kit items, or accessories for each device.

If your organization maintains more than one AED, record the AED location or device number in the second column to ensure clear tracking.

Date	AED Location / Device ID	Item Replaced	Reason for Replacement	Replaced By (Name / Initials)	Next Replacement Due	Remarks

(Tip: Record pad expirations, battery replacements, alarm battery changes, and rescue kit restocks here. For multi-AED campuses, assign a simple device label such as "AED #1—Front Lobby," "AED #2—2nd Floor Hallway," etc.)

Replacement Log

Use this page to record every replacement or update of AED components, including pads, batteries, rescue kit items, or accessories for each device.

If your organization maintains more than one AED, record the AED location or device number in the second column to ensure clear tracking.

Date	AED Location / Device ID	Item Replaced	Reason for Replacement	Replaced By (Name / Initials)	Next Replacement Due	Remarks

(Tip: Record pad expirations, battery replacements, alarm battery changes, and rescue kit restocks here. For multi-AED campuses, assign a simple device label such as "AED #1—Front Lobby," "AED #2—2nd Floor Hallway," etc.)

Replacement Log

Use this page to record every replacement or update of AED components, including pads, batteries, rescue kit items, or accessories for each device.

If your organization maintains more than one AED, record the AED location or device number in the second column to ensure clear tracking.

Date	AED Location / Device ID	Item Replaced	Reason for Replacement	Replaced By (Name / Initials)	Next Replacement Due	Remarks

(Tip: Record pad expirations, battery replacements, alarm battery changes, and rescue kit restocks here. For multi-AED campuses, assign a simple device label such as "AED #1—Front Lobby," "AED #2—2nd Floor Hallway," etc.)

Replacement Log

Use this page to record every replacement or update of AED components, including pads, batteries, rescue kit items, or accessories for each device.

If your organization maintains more than one AED, record the AED location or device number in the second column to ensure clear tracking.

Date	AED Location / Device ID	Item Replaced	Reason for Replacement	Replaced By (Name / Initials)	Next Replacement Due	Remarks

(Tip: Record pad expirations, battery replacements, alarm battery changes, and rescue kit restocks here. For multi-AED campuses, assign a simple device label such as "AED #1—Front Lobby," "AED #2—2nd Floor Hallway," etc.)

Replacement Log

Use this page to record every replacement or update of AED components, including pads, batteries, rescue kit items, or accessories for each device.
If your organization maintains more than one AED, record the AED location or device number in the second column to ensure clear tracking.

Date	AED Location / Device ID	Item Replaced	Reason for Replacement	Replaced By (Name / Initials)	Next Replacement Due	Remarks

(Tip: Record pad expirations, battery replacements, alarm battery changes, and rescue kit restocks here. For multi-AED campuses, assign a simple device label such as "AED #1—Front Lobby," "AED #2—2nd Floor Hallway," etc.)

Replacement Log

Use this page to record every replacement or update of AED components, including pads, batteries, rescue kit items, or accessories for each device.

If your organization maintains more than one AED, record the AED location or device number in the second column to ensure clear tracking.

Date	AED Location / Device ID	Item Replaced	Reason for Replacement	Replaced By (Name / Initials)	Next Replacement Due	Remarks

(Tip: Record pad expirations, battery replacements, alarm battery changes, and rescue kit restocks here. For multi-AED campuses, assign a simple device label such as "AED #1—Front Lobby," "AED #2—2nd Floor Hallway," etc.)

Notes

Notes

Troubleshooting Notes

Use this page to document any issues, malfunctions, or maintenance concerns identified during inspection. Recording corrective actions ensures accountability and provides a maintenance history for audits and future reference.

Date	AED Location / Device ID	Issue Found	Reported By (Name/ Initials)	Corrective Action Taken	Follow-up Required (Y/N)	Resolved By/Date	Notes

(Attach copies of any service reports or photos of repairs as needed.)

Troubleshooting Notes

Use this page to document any issues, malfunctions, or maintenance concerns identified during inspection. Recording corrective actions ensures accountability and provides a maintenance history for audits and future reference.

Date	AED Location / Device ID	Issue Found	Reported By (Name/ Initials)	Corrective Action Taken	Follow-up Required (Y/N)	Resolved By/Date	Notes

(Attach copies of any service reports or photos of repairs as needed.)

Troubleshooting Notes

Use this page to document any issues, malfunctions, or maintenance concerns identified during inspection. Recording corrective actions ensures accountability and provides a maintenance history for audits and future reference.

Date	AED Location / Device ID	Issue Found	Reported By (Name/ Initials)	Corrective Action Taken	Follow-up Required (Y/N)	Resolved By/Date	Notes

(Attach copies of any service reports or photos of repairs as needed.)

Troubleshooting Notes

Use this page to document any issues, malfunctions, or maintenance concerns identified during inspection. Recording corrective actions ensures accountability and provides a maintenance history for audits and future reference.

Date	AED Location / Device ID	Issue Found	Reported By (Name/ Initials)	Corrective Action Taken	Follow-up Required (Y/N)	Resolved By/Date	Notes

(Attach copies of any service reports or photos of repairs as needed.)

Troubleshooting Notes

Use this page to document any issues, malfunctions, or maintenance concerns identified during inspection. Recording corrective actions ensures accountability and provides a maintenance history for audits and future reference.

Date	AED Location / Device ID	Issue Found	Reported By (Name/ Initials)	Corrective Action Taken	Follow-up Required (Y/N)	Resolved By/Date	Notes

(Attach copies of any service reports or photos of repairs as needed.)

Troubleshooting Notes

Use this page to document any issues, malfunctions, or maintenance concerns identified during inspection. Recording corrective actions ensures accountability and provides a maintenance history for audits and future reference.

Date	AED Location / Device ID	Issue Found	Reported By (Name/ Initials)	Corrective Action Taken	Follow-up Required (Y/N)	Resolved By/Date	Notes

(Attach copies of any service reports or photos of repairs as needed.)

Troubleshooting Notes

Use this page to document any issues, malfunctions, or maintenance concerns identified during inspection. Recording corrective actions ensures accountability and provides a maintenance history for audits and future reference.

Date	AED Location / Device ID	Issue Found	Reported By (Name/ Initials)	Corrective Action Taken	Follow-up Required (Y/N)	Resolved By/Date	Notes

(Attach copies of any service reports or photos of repairs as needed.)

Troubleshooting Notes

Use this page to document any issues, malfunctions, or maintenance concerns identified during inspection. Recording corrective actions ensures accountability and provides a maintenance history for audits and future reference.

Date	AED Location / Device ID	Issue Found	Reported By (Name/ Initials)	Corrective Action Taken	Follow-up Required (Y/N)	Resolved By/Date	Notes

(Attach copies of any service reports or photos of repairs as needed.)

Troubleshooting Notes

Use this page to document any issues, malfunctions, or maintenance concerns identified during inspection. Recording corrective actions ensures accountability and provides a maintenance history for audits and future reference.

Date	AED Location / Device ID	Issue Found	Reported By (Name/ Initials)	Corrective Action Taken	Follow-up Required (Y/N)	Resolved By/Date	Notes

(Attach copies of any service reports or photos of repairs as needed.)

Notes

Annual AED Inspection Summary

This page provides a year-end summary of your facilitiy's AED maintenance record. Use it to verify that all inspections have been completed, issues resolved, and supplies remain in compliance. This page should be reviewed and signed by the Safety Coordinator or AED Program Leader each year.

Year: ____________________ **AED Location/Device ID:** ____________________

Month	Inspection Completed (Y/N)	Inspector's Initials	Issues Found	Date Resolved	Verified By Coordinator (Y/N)
January					
February					
March					
April					
May					
June					
July					
August					
September					
October					
November					
December					

Review Date	Reviewed By (Name & Title)	Signature	Remarks / Next Steps

End of Year Verification

- All inspections completed and documented.
- Replacement parts and batteries updated.
- AED rescue kit checked and completed.
- AED program remains compliant and operational.

Signature (Safety Coordinator): ______________________________

Date: ______________________

Annual AED Inspection Summary

This page provides a year-end summary of your church's AED maintenance record. Use it to verify that all inspections have been completed, issues resolved, and supplies remain in compliance. This page should be reviewed and signed by the Safety Coordinator or AED Program Leader each year.

Year: ____________________ **AED Location/Device ID:** ____________________

Month	Inspection Completed (Y/N)	Inspector's Initials	Issues Found	Date Resolved	Verified By Coordinator (Y/N)
January					
February					
March					
April					
May					
June					
July					
August					
September					
October					
November					
December					

Review Date	Reviewed By (Name & Title)	Signature	Remarks / Next Steps

End of Year Verification

- All inspections completed and documented.
- Replacement parts and batteries updated.
- AED rescue kit checked and completed.
- AED program remains compliant and operational.

Signature (Safety Coordinator): ______________________________

Date: ____________________

Annual AED Inspection Summary

This page provides a year-end summary of your church's AED maintenance record. Use it to verify that all inspections have been completed, issues resolved, and supplies remain in compliance. This page should be reviewed and signed by the Safety Coordinator or AED Program Leader each year.

Year: ______________________ **AED Location/Device ID:** ______________________

Month	Inspection Completed (Y/N)	Inspector's Initials	Issues Found	Date Resolved	Verified By Coordinator (Y/N)
January					
February					
March					
April					
May					
June					
July					
August					
September					
October					
November					
December					

Review Date	Reviewed By (Name & Title)	Signature	Remarks / Next Steps

End of Year Verification

- All inspections completed and documented.
- Replacement parts and batteries updated.
- AED rescue kit checked and completed.
- AED program remains compliant and operational.

Signature (Safety Coordinator): ______________________________

Date: ______________________

Annual AED Inspection Summary

This page provides a year-end summary of your church's AED maintenance record. Use it to verify that all inspections have been completed, issues resolved, and supplies remain in compliance. This page should be reviewed and signed by the Safety Coordinator or AED Program Leader each year.

Year: ______________________ **AED Location/Device ID:** ______________________

Month	Inspection Completed (Y/N)	Inspector's Initials	Issues Found	Date Resolved	Verified By Coordinator (Y/N)
January					
February					
March					
April					
May					
June					
July					
August					
September					
October					
November					
December					

Review Date	Reviewed By (Name & Title)	Signature	Remarks / Next Steps

End of Year Verification

- All inspections completed and documented.
- Replacement parts and batteries updated.
- AED rescue kit checked and completed.
- AED program remains compliant and operational.

Signature (Safety Coordinator): ______________________________
Date: ______________________

Annual AED Inspection Summary

This page provides a year-end summary of your church's AED maintenance record. Use it to verify that all inspections have been completed, issues resolved, and supplies remain in compliance. This page should be reviewed and signed by the Safety Coordinator or AED Program Leader each year.

Year: ______________________ **AED Location/Device ID:** ______________________

Month	Inspection Completed (Y/N)	Inspector's Initials	Issues Found	Date Resolved	Verified By Coordinator (Y/N)
January					
February					
March					
April					
May					
June					
July					
August					
September					
October					
November					
December					

Review Date	Reviewed By (Name & Title)	Signature	Remarks / Next Steps

End of Year Verification

- All inspections completed and documented.
- Replacement parts and batteries updated.
- AED rescue kit checked and completed.
- AED program remains compliant and operational.

Signature (Safety Coordinator): ______________________________

Date: ______________________

Annual AED Inspection Summary

This page provides a year-end summary of your church's AED maintenance record. Use it to verify that all inspections have been completed, issues resolved, and supplies remain in compliance. This page should be reviewed and signed by the Safety Coordinator or AED Program Leader each year.

Year: ______________________ **AED Location/Device ID:** ______________________

Month	Inspection Completed (Y/N)	Inspector's Initials	Issues Found	Date Resolved	Verified By Coordinator (Y/N)
January					
February					
March					
April					
May					
June					
July					
August					
September					
October					
November					
December					

Review Date	Reviewed By (Name & Title)	Signature	Remarks / Next Steps

End of Year Verification

- All inspections completed and documented.
- Replacement parts and batteries updated.
- AED rescue kit checked and completed.
- AED program remains compliant and operational.

Signature (Safety Coordinator): ______________________________

Date: ______________________

Annual AED Inspection Summary

This page provides a year-end summary of your church's AED maintenance record. Use it to verify that all inspections have been completed, issues resolved, and supplies remain in compliance. This page should be reviewed and signed by the Safety Coordinator or AED Program Leader each year.

Year: ______________________ **AED Location/Device ID:** ______________________

Month	Inspection Completed (Y/N)	Inspector's Initials	Issues Found	Date Resolved	Verified By Coordinator (Y/N)
January					
February					
March					
April					
May					
June					
July					
August					
September					
October					
November					
December					

Review Date	Reviewed By (Name & Title)	Signature	Remarks / Next Steps

End of Year Verification

- All inspections completed and documented.
- Replacement parts and batteries updated.
- AED rescue kit checked and completed.
- AED program remains compliant and operational.

Signature (Safety Coordinator): ______________________________

Date: ______________________

Annual AED Inspection Summary

This page provides a year-end summary of your church's AED maintenance record. Use it to verify that all inspections have been completed, issues resolved, and supplies remain in compliance. This page should be reviewed and signed by the Safety Coordinator or AED Program Leader each year.

Year: ______________________ **AED Location/Device ID:** ______________________

Month	Inspection Completed (Y/N)	Inspector's Initials	Issues Found	Date Resolved	Verified By Coordinator (Y/N)
January					
February					
March					
April					
May					
June					
July					
August					
September					
October					
November					
December					

Review Date	Reviewed By (Name & Title)	Signature	Remarks / Next Steps

End of Year Verification

- All inspections completed and documented.
- Replacement parts and batteries updated.
- AED rescue kit checked and completed.
- AED program remains compliant and operational.

Signature (Safety Coordinator): ______________________________

Date: ______________________

Annual AED Inspection Summary

This page provides a year-end summary of your church's AED maintenance record. Use it to verify that all inspections have been completed, issues resolved, and supplies remain in compliance. This page should be reviewed and signed by the Safety Coordinator or AED Program Leader each year.

Year: ______________________ **AED Location/Device ID:** ______________________

Month	Inspection Completed (Y/N)	Inspector's Initials	Issues Found	Date Resolved	Verified By Coordinator (Y/N)
January					
February					
March					
April					
May					
June					
July					
August					
September					
October					
November					
December					

Review Date	Reviewed By (Name & Title)	Signature	Remarks / Next Steps

End of Year Verification

- All inspections completed and documented.
- Replacement parts and batteries updated.
- AED rescue kit checked and completed.
- AED program remains compliant and operational.

Signature (Safety Coordinator): ______________________________

Date: ______________________

Annual AED Inspection Summary

This page provides a year-end summary of your church's AED maintenance record. Use it to verify that all inspections have been completed, issues resolved, and supplies remain in compliance. This page should be reviewed and signed by the Safety Coordinator or AED Program Leader each year.

Year: ______________________ **AED Location/Device ID:** ______________________

Month	Inspection Completed (Y/N)	Inspector's Initials	Issues Found	Date Resolved	Verified By Coordinator (Y/N)
January					
February					
March					
April					
May					
June					
July					
August					
September					
October					
November					
December					

Review Date	Reviewed By (Name & Title)	Signature	Remarks / Next Steps

End of Year Verification

- All inspections completed and documented.
- Replacement parts and batteries updated.
- AED rescue kit checked and completed.
- AED program remains compliant and operational.

Signature (Safety Coordinator): ______________________________

Date: ______________________

Annual AED Inspection Summary

This page provides a year-end summary of your church's AED maintenance record. Use it to verify that all inspections have been completed, issues resolved, and supplies remain in compliance. This page should be reviewed and signed by the Safety Coordinator or AED Program Leader each year.

Year: ____________________ **AED Location/Device ID:** ____________________

Month	Inspection Completed (Y/N)	Inspector's Initials	Issues Found	Date Resolved	Verified By Coordinator (Y/N)
January					
February					
March					
April					
May					
June					
July					
August					
September					
October					
November					
December					

Review Date	Reviewed By (Name & Title)	Signature	Remarks / Next Steps

End of Year Verification

- All inspections completed and documented.
- Replacement parts and batteries updated.
- AED rescue kit checked and completed.
- AED program remains compliant and operational.

Signature (Safety Coordinator): ______________________________

Date: ______________________

Annual AED Inspection Summary

This page provides a year-end summary of your church's AED maintenance record. Use it to verify that all inspections have been completed, issues resolved, and supplies remain in compliance. This page should be reviewed and signed by the Safety Coordinator or AED Program Leader each year.

Year: ______________________ **AED Location/Device ID:** ________________________

Month	Inspection Completed (Y/N)	Inspector's Initials	Issues Found	Date Resolved	Verified By Coordinator (Y/N)
January					
February					
March					
April					
May					
June					
July					
August					
September					
October					
November					
December					

Review Date	Reviewed By (Name & Title)	Signature	Remarks / Next Steps

End of Year Verification

- All inspections completed and documented.
- Replacement parts and batteries updated.
- AED rescue kit checked and completed.
- AED program remains compliant and operational.

Signature (Safety Coordinator): ________________________________

Date: ________________________

Notes

Notes

Closing Message

Emergency preparedness is not a single decision. It is a process maintained over time.

Regular inspections, clear documentation, and responsible equipment management help ensure that lifesaving devices remain ready if an emergency occurs.

By maintaining accurate records, organizations demonstrate a commitment to protecting employees, visitors, and members of the public.

Consistent AED readiness helps ensure that when every second matters, the equipment is prepared to perform as intended.

About the Author

Ebony Godwin, RN, BSN, M.S., is a registered nurse, CPR instructor, and emergency preparedness educator. She works with organizations, schools, and community groups to improve emergency readiness through training, equipment placement, and practical safety systems.

Through her work with Hospital Med Supply, Ebony helps workplaces and community organizations implement Automated External Defibrillator (AED) programs and maintain readiness through proper inspection, documentation, and training.

The DigiMedical logbook series was created to provide practical tools that help organizations maintain clear records, support safety programs, and keep lifesaving equipment ready when it matters most.

Share Your Experience

If you've used this logbook as part of your facility's AED maintenance or readiness efforts, you may choose to share your experience.

Reviews help other organizational leaders understand how this resource supports emergency preparedness.

If you purchased this book through an online retailer, you may choose to leave a review on that website.

If you received this book directly through your organization or a direct order, your feedback is still valued.

Thank you for taking the time to share your experience and for your commitment to caring well for the people entrusted to your care.

Notes

Notes

Made in United States
North Haven, CT
05 November 2026

21767246R00046